Also available in this series from Quadrille:

MINDFULNESS
QUIET
FRIENDSHIP
LOVE
CONFIDENCE
TIDINESS
HAPPINESS
US
MINDFULNESS II
MOTHERHOOD
LUCK
SEX
CHRISTMAS
SELF-CARE
SISTERHOOD
KINDNESS
BRIDESMAIDS
PRIDE
GRATITUDE
POSITIVITY
UNITY
HOPE
JOY
COURAGE
MANIFESTING
SELF-LOVE
RESILIENCE
EMPOWERMENT
FOCUS
REST

the little book of

PRAYER

Quadrille

About prayer

Why pray? Why meditate? Why seek the divine? In our materialist world, we have come to expect rational explanations of mysteries and precise conceptions of the truth, but we are often left wanting more. Whether you're a believer in God or seeking a deeper experience of life, the practice of daily prayer can be transformative. We are encouraged to open our hearts and minds to the possibility of a connection with the divine. Find a quiet space and listen. Use the prayers within the little book to begin a lifelong conversation with your own conscience – and ultimately with God.

About Christianity

Just over 2,000 years ago, Jesus preached in the lands of Galilee. His message concerned forgiveness, and he commanded people to love one another. He healed the sick and thousands followed him. Jesus Christ (the Anointed One) was crucified, his body disappeared from the tomb and his disciples testified that he rose from the dead. Accounts of Christ's life were written shortly after his death and resurrection, and the gospel (good news) spread across the Roman Empire. All of the disciples were martyred for their faith.

Today there are approximately 2.4 billion Christians. Christ taught us that this life on Earth is not all there is, and that if we love one another and ask forgiveness for our sins, we will enter into everlasting life. Prayer is the method Jesus taught to bridge this world and the heavenly realm.

Some of the archaic language has been updated to make it clearer for the modern reader.

What is prayer?

Definition:

noun

1. The words someone says or thinks when they are praying.
2. The act or ceremony in which someone prays.
3. The act or ceremony of speaking to God, especially to express thanks or to ask for help.

The word pray derives from
the Latin word *precari*, meaning
'to ask earnestly, beg, entreat'.

When the disciples asked Jesus how to pray, he taught them The Lord's Prayer. This prayer has been spoken by followers of Christ since the 1st century. When saying The Lord's Prayer we join this reverent chain of wisdom; from Jesus's lips to our own.

The Lord's Prayer

Our Father who art in heaven,
hallowed be thy name;
thy kingdom come;
thy will be done;
on earth as it is in heaven.
Give us this day our daily bread.
And forgive us our trespasses,
as we forgive those who trespass
against us.

And lead us not into temptation,
but deliver us from evil.
For thine is the kingdom,
the power and the glory,
for ever and ever.
Amen.

Use the Lord's Prayer as a map to a prayerful life

- Recite the Lord's Prayer line by line.
- Listen to your heart: let it be stirred and moved by the words.
- After each line, meditate on the sense of the words.
- With the meanings absorbed, pray that you are able enact the spirit of the prayer.

"The Lord's Prayer is the most perfect of prayers... In it we ask, not only for all the things we can rightly desire, but also in the sequence that they should be desired. This prayer not only teaches us to ask for things, but also in what order we should desire them."

SAINT THOMAS AQUINAS

Prayer is communing with God

Consider how profound a notion this is: prayer is communing with the divinity. To pray is not merely to say daily mantras or affirmations. To pray is not merely speaking into the void or to your own personal brick wall. To pray is to commune with God. Prayer is therefore a two-way conversation.

“Prayer is not the reverberation of sound; it is the articulation of love. It is with the heart rather than the lips that we pray… Therefore whether we cry to the Lord with voice of the body – where occasion demands it – or in the silence, we must cry from the heart.”

SAINT AUGUSTINE

Prayer is the little implement
Through which Men reach
Where Presence – is denied them.
They fling their Speech

By means of it – in God's Ear –
If then He hear –
This sums the Apparatus
Comprised in Prayer –

EMILY DICKINSON
Prayer Is the Little Implement

"Prayer does not mean simply to pour out one's heart. It means rather to find the way to God and to speak with him, whether the heart is full or empty."

DIETRICH BONHOEFFER

"Pray often, because prayer is a shield to the soul."

JOHN BUNYAN

Open, O doors and bolts of my heart, that Christ the King of Glory may enter!

Enter, O my Light, and enlighten my darkness;

Enter, O my Life, and resurrect my deadness;

Enter, O my Physician, and heal my wounds;

Enter, O Divine Fire, and burn up the thorns of my sins;

Ignite my inward parts and my heart with the flame of Your love;

Enter, O my King, and destroy
in me the kingdom of sin;

Sit on the throne of my heart and
alone reign in me, O Thou,
my King and Lord!

SAINT DIMITRI OF ROSTOV

"Prayer is a humble request either of the heart, or tongue, or both to God, proceeding from our belief and acknowledgment of his power, as God, and of his goodness, as our Father in Jesus Christ, to supply all our needs, with thanksgiving to him for any blessing received.

The parts of a Prayer are usually three:

1. *Humble confession.*
2. *Petition or supplication.*
3. *Hearty thanksgiving."*

JOHN COLET

How to pray

A suggestion for intentional prayer practice:

1. Settle yourself.
2. Sit with an upright back.
3. Take five or six deep breaths.
4. Focus on the word *God*.
5. Relax into the prayer.

A simple way to enter prayer

"Kneel or stand with your hands folded and your eyes towards heaven and think or speak as briefly as you can."

MARTIN LUTHER

Aim for consistency. Dedicating only five minutes a day to prayer will evolve into a daily habit. If you are finding the experience of short prayer beneficial, consider gently extending the prayer time and deepening your communion with God. Aim for consistency.

Consistent prayer does not help God hear us, but helps us hear God.

A short prayer for inner peace

Lord, tune our hearts to love and then give us an inward peace, a restfulness about everything.

CHARLES SPURGEON

Use your body to pray

Experiment with different ways of using your body to help your soul. With your hands together, or open in a pleading condition; your eyes open or closed; your mouth speaking, singing or being silent; your body kneeling, standing or prostrating, still or gently swaying.

With a reverent attitude in whatever form, your body will teach you the best means of helping your soul to find its path to prayerful energy.

We are encouraged by Saint Paul to 'pray without ceasing.' Quite a task. What can it mean?

Rejoice always!
Pray constantly.
Give thanks in everything.

The call to pray constantly can be understood to mean we should recollect God in our ordinary comings and goings. To remember God at all times will help us to act kindly to others and ourselves. In this instance prayer is less about a list of wants, and more about a constant loving state of mind.

Learn by heart the *Agnus Dei* – 'Lamb of God' – and meditate on the concept that Jesus died so we may live.

Lamb of God, you take away the
sin of the world, have mercy on us.

Lamb of God, you take away the
sin of the world, have mercy on us.

Lamb of God, you take away the
sin of the world, grant us peace.

What's the difference between vocal and internal prayer?

Vocal prayer involves reading or reciting prayers written by others, based on Biblical texts or prayers from holy men and women. Vocal prayers can fill those praying with confidence that they have been said by holy men and women for centuries.

Internal prayer involves a direct communion with our own soul and God. These prayers can be less formal, as emotional longings from the heart.

Experiment with both practices to find out which delivers peace and spiritual elevation.

Saint Catherine, a medieval mystic, described how, when praying, her heart became 'inebriated... on fire with love.'

Why should ecstatic prayer be a thing that is experienced only by ancient saints? Give yourself permission to allow prayer to infuse your whole nervous system.

"Oh! Eternal God! Oh! Light above every other light, from whom issues all light! Oh! Fire above every fire, because you are the only fire who burn without consuming, and consume all sin and self-love found in the soul, not afflicting her, but fattening her with insatiable love, and though the soul is filled she is not sated, but ever desires you, and the more of you she has, the more she seeks – and the more she desires, the more she finds and tastes of you – supreme and eternal fire."

SAINT CATHERINE OF SIENA

“Pray night and day very quietly, like a little, weary child, for everything you want, in body as well as in soul – the least thing as well as the greatest – nothing is too much to ask God for – nothing too great for him to grant – and try to thank him for everything. Glory be to you, O God!”

CHARLES KINGSLEY

"Prayer needs no teacher. It requires diligence, effort and personal ardour, and then God will be its teacher."

SAINT MELETIUS THE CONFESSOR

"Let nothing disturb you,
Let nothing frighten you,
All things are passing away:
God never changes.
Patience obtains all things.
Whoever has God lacks nothing;
God alone suffices."

SAINT TERESA OF ÁVILA

Prayer is a wild invitation to ask God to fill you with divine energy.

"*How much more will the heavenly Father give the Holy Spirit to those who ask him.*"

LUKE, 11:13,
ENGLISH STANDARD VERSION

The Eastern Orthodox Church encourages the use of icons to support the path of prayer. Whether in a church, or placed reverentially in the corner of your home, the icon acts as a divine focus. Rather than closing your eyes, pray with open eyes before a holy icon of Christ or Mary, the Mother of God. This helps to prevent wandering off into daydreams or fantasies by focusing instead on Jesus or Mary.

Inspirational prayer practice from the Orthodox tradition

1. Pray East towards a holy icon.
2. Light a candle.
3. Bow three times to the icon.
4. Breathe deeply.
5. Stand and settle your weight well.
6. Make the sign of the cross three times while saying: *Holy God, Holy Mighty, Holy Immortal: have mercy on us.*

"Prayer is the refuge of help, a source of salvation, a treasury of assurance, a haven that rescues from the tempest, a light to those who are in darkness, a staff of the infirm, a shelter in time of temptations, a medicine at the height of sickness, a shield of deliverance in war, an arrow sharpened against the face of the enemies, to speak simply: the entire multitude of these good things is found to have its entrance through prayer."

SAINT ISAAC THE SYRIAN

Take, Lord, and receive all my liberty,
my memory, my understanding,
and my entire will,
All I have and call my own.
You have given all to me.
To you, Lord, I return it.
Everything is yours;
do with it what you will.
Give me only your love and your grace,
that is enough for me.

SAINT IGATIUS
Surrender Prayer

“To sing is to pray twice.”

SAINT AUGUSTINE

“Where there is devotional music, God is always at hand with his gracious presence.”

JOHANN SEBASTIAN BACH

Music and prayer

Just as Jesus sang hymns with his disciples, embrace the use of music to enter a state of prayer.

1. Choose music that matches the rhythm of your heart.
2. Immerse yourself in the beauty of the piece and let your surroundings seep away.
3. Breathe deeply.
4. Begin your approach to the Lord.

How to frame our heart and mind in readiness for conversation with God

1. If buzzing with the demands of the day, write a list of things large and small that need addressing. Remove them temporarily from your mind.
2. Find a quiet place.
3. Light a candle.
4. Deep breathe for as long as needed to help your heart find stillness.
5. Close your eyes.
6. Take comfort in the knowledge that the Lord knows you are there.

Discover the ancient practice of *Lectio Divina* – the divine reading of holy texts

1. ***Lectio*** (read): read the passage again and again, slowly, contemplating each word and hearing which words or passages resonate and speak to you.
2. ***Meditatio*** (meditate): ponder upon the words or phrases and consider how they may apply to your life.

3. ***Oratio*** (pray): begin a conversation with God about the text you are thinking about.
4. ***Contemplatio*** (contemplate): being still in God's presence, move beyond the textual word to silent absorption of what the passage means for your spirit and your actions.

Take small steps

Francis de Sales gently teaches the spiritually hungry how to pray and commune with God. He begins by suggesting very small steps:

Preparation

1. Place yourself in the presence of God.
2. Ask him to inspire your heart.

"My arms have clasped you
and should set you free,
But no, I cannot let you go!
You dwell within my heart.
Lord Jesus Christ, Beloved,
tell, O tell me true,
What shall your servant do?"

NARAYAN VAMAN TILAK

Lord my God, full of mercy and pity, I appeal to you, I flee to you, I rest in you. Though weak and unable to stand in your presence, yet let your spirit of strength hold me up. Say to me, 'Fear not, for my Grace is sufficient for you, my child.'

FROM 17TH-CENTURY
DAILY DEVOTIONS

*“ Draw near to God,
and he will draw near to you.”*

JAMES, 4:8,
ENGLISH STANDARD VERSION

Remember these words when trying to pray – simply orientating your mind towards the divine is sufficient for a growing closeness with God.

Prayer invites everyone to pursue knowledge of the Lord. This knowledge doesn't need to be heavy, difficult study, but a simple *knowing* that God is there.

"Let us know, let us pursue knowledge of the Lord."

HOSEA, 6:3,
INTERNATIONAL STANDARD VERSION

"Then Mary took a whole pint of a very expensive perfume made of pure nard, poured it on Jesus' feet, and wiped them with her hair. The sweet smell of the perfume filled the whole house."

JOHN, 12:3,
GOOD NEWS BIBLE

Mary anointed Jesus's feet with lavishly expensive perfume, so much so that its aroma filled the whole house. This immersive act can inform prayerful practice. Be inspired by Mary and use scents and perfumes to further deepen the sensory experience of prayer.

"May my prayer be like special perfume before You. May the lifting up of my hands be like the evening gift given on the altar in worship."

PSALM 141, VERSE 2,
NEW LIVING TRANSLATION

Perfume and prayer

Prayer has been called 'the incense of our hearts.' When praying, imagine your prayers rising like sweet-smelling incense towards the divine. Using incense while praying at home can help foster a prayerful and reverent state of mind.

“Pray all the time. Ask God for anything in line with the Holy Spirit’s wishes. Plead with him, reminding him of your needs, and keep praying earnestly for all Christians everywhere.”

EPHESIANS, 6:18,
NEW LIVING TRANSLATION

"Dear Lord, who does give peace, shed down upon us all your holy calm. Gather together with your hand all those who are scattered, and bring them like sheep into the fold of your holy church, through Jesus Christ our Lord."

THEODORUS STUDITA

Holy calm

Pray and consider deeply the concept of 'holy calm' as used by Theodorus Studita, a Byzantine monk from the 9th century. What does 'holy calm' mean to you? Are you able to seek and maintain 'holy calm' during moments of high stress and prolonged times of challenge? Begin by cultivating 'holy calm' when already in a state of happy peace.

Prayer is often experienced in the darkness behind our eyes. The idea of light, of dawn, of illumination coming through the shadows of our own fears is powerful.

"The Dawn from on high will visit us to shine on those who live in darkness and the shadow of death, to guide our feet into the way of peace."

LUKE, 1:78–79,
HOLMAN BIBLE

A blessing for illumination

May the light of Christ, the King of all, shine ever brighter in our hearts, that with all the saints in light we may shine forth as lights in the world.

Discover the ARRR form of prayer

Acknowledge – acknowledge that you are in the presence of divine majesty.

Relate – relate everything to God that is in your heart, no matter how difficult.

Receive – receive God's response. Listen, wait and accept the messages God sends.

Respond – respond to the prayer's revelation.

*"I will pray with my spirit,
but I will pray with my mind also;
I will sing praise with my spirit,
but I will sing with my mind also."*

1 CORINTHIANS, 14:15,
ENGLISH STANDARD VERSION

We are promised that when a small number of people come together to pray, God will be there. Draw strength from praying with others in the company of God.

"For where two or three are gathered in my name, there am I among them."

MATTHEW, 18:20,
ENGLISH STANDARD VERSION

Sometimes it can feel greedy or grasping to pray. Too much: I want... help me... I need this. But fear not, Christians are instructed to give their fears to God. Ask away!

"Do not be anxious about anything, but in every situation, by prayer and petition, with thanksgiving, present your requests to God. And the peace of God, which transcends all understanding, will guard your hearts and your minds in Christ Jesus."

SAINT PAUL WRITING TO
THE PHILIPPIANS, 4:6–7,
NEW INTERNATIONAL VERSION

Be encouraged that your needs will be met.

"But my God shall supply all your need according to his riches in glory by Christ Jesus."

SAINT PAUL WRITING TO
THE PHILIPPIANS, 4:19
NEW INTERNATIONAL VERSION

Inspired by the disciples who prayed together for nine days after Jesus had ascended into heaven, a tradition of *novena* was developed.

Novena, from the Latin for nine, involves the practice of praying intentionally for nine days in a row. Repeated requests are made for guidance or healing, and the repetition of the prayers helps foster confidence in praying within a clear structure.

On the tenth day of praying, the disciples received the Holy Spirit, an event that is celebrated every year at Pentecost.

A novena to the Holy Spirit: pray it every day for nine days

Come, Holy Spirit!

Fall afresh on Your people

Purify and cleanse us

Open our hearts to receive Your gifts

So that we may be born again in You.

Amen.

Do not be surprised by the extraordinary power of prayer!

"As the believers met together that day, suddenly there was a sound like the roaring of a mighty windstorm in the skies above them and it filled the house where they were meeting. Then, what looked like flames or tongues of fire appeared and settled on their heads. And everyone present was filled with the Holy Spirit."

ACTS, 2:1–4,
LIVING BIBLE

O holy comforter, sweetest consolation of the sorrowful, gracious holy spirit come down at this time with your mighty power into the depths of our hearts. Gladden there with your brightness every dark retreat, and enrich all with the dew of your abundant comfort. Kindle our inward parts with holy favour, that the incense of our prayers and praises may ever go up to you, our God; through Jesus Christ your son our Lord. Amen.

SAINT ANSELM

“About three in the morning as we were continuing instant in prayer, the power of God came mightily upon us, insomuch that many cried out for exceeding joy, and many fell to the ground. As soon as we recovered a little from the awe and amazement at the presence of His Majesty, we broke out with one voice, ‘We praise Thee, O God, we acknowledge Thee to be the Lord.’”

JOHN WESLEY
Describing an encounter with God after a long period of communal prayer

Dear Lord, give us, we beseech you, in the name of Jesus Christ, that love which can never cease, that will kindle our lamps but not extinguish them, that they may burn in us and enlighten others. Lord Jesus, we pray you may give your light to our lamps, that in its light the most holy place may be revealed to us in which you dwell, that we may always behold you, desire you, look upon you in love, and long after you, for your sake.

SAINT COLUMBA

"When I rose from my knees, there seemed a voice speaking to me... 'Ask for sanctification.' ... I again bowed in the same place... and said, 'Lord, sanctify my soul for Christ's sake.' That very instant, as if lightning had darted through me, I sprang to my feet, and cried, 'The Lord has sanctified my soul!'"

JARENA LEE

My Lord God, my all in all, life of my life and spirit of my spirit, look in mercy upon me and so fill me with your holy spirit that my heart shall have no room for love of anything else but you. Take away then from my heart all that is opposed to you and enter and abide and rule forever, Amen.

SADHU SUNDAR SINGH

Bring us, O Lord God, at our
last awakening
Into the house and gate of heaven,
To enter into that gate and dwell
in that house,
Where there shall be no darkness
nor dazzling,
But one equal light; no noise nor
silence, but one equal music;
No fears or hopes, but one
equal possession;
No ends or beginnings, but one
equal eternity,
In the habitations of thy glory and
dominion, world without end.

JOHN DONNE

Using prayerful poems is a time-honoured method of enhancing prayer. Alight on the blissful language and piercing concepts, and meditate on images that inspire curiosity and a longing for more. Using John Donne's prayer, consider deeply what these beautiful ideas mean to you.

One equal music
One equal possession
One equal eternity

Explore prayer prompts to inspire divine communication

- Dear Lord I thank you for...
- Christ Jesus I am grateful towards...
- My Father I am fearful of...
- Holy Spirit guide me towards...
- God in heaven protect me from...

Morning and evening prayers

Develop habitual prayer practices by dedicating specific times of the day to orient your soul towards God. Traditionally, morning, noon and night match the natural rhythms of the day.

- Morning to make prayerful commitments.
- Noon to pause and gather your scattered senses.
- Evening to give praise and thanks.

In the evening and morning and
noonday we praise you, we thank you,
and pray you, master of all, to direct
our prayers as incense before you.
Let not our hearts turn away to words
or thoughts of faults, but keep us
from all things that might hurt us;
for to you, O Lord, our eyes look up,
and our hope is in you: confuse us not,
O our God; for the sake of Jesus Christ
our Lord. Amen.

ANCIENT EASTERN CHURCH VESPERS

A small something to say at the start of prayer

As I begin to pray now, I pause to be still; to breathe slowly, to re-centre my scattered senses upon the presence of God.

If seeking to anchor daily prayer using a centuries old, well-tested method, The Book of Common Prayer includes prayers for morning and evening. Said every day, they have brought peace and joy to millions of believers.

"We praise you O God: we acknowledge you to be the Lord."

THE BOOK OF COMMON PRAYER

A Collect for Grace in Morning Prayer

O Lord, our heavenly Father, Almighty and everlasting God, who has safely brought us to the beginning of this day. Defend us in the same with your mighty power; and grant that this day we fall into no error, neither run into any kind of danger, but that all our doings may be ordered by your governance, to do always what is right in your sight; through Jesus Christ our Lord, Amen.

THE BOOK OF COMMON PRAYER

A simple prayer at the start of the day

Lord Jesus Christ, help us to do what is right in your sight. Amen.

A morning prayer by Saint Thérèse of Lisieux

O my God! I offer you all my actions of this day for the intentions and for the glory of the sacred heart of Jesus. I desire to sanctify every beat of my heart, my every thought, my simplest works, by uniting them to your infinite merits.

Try to memorize a prayer opening that has been spoken by the holy for millennia.

"To You, O Lord, I lift up my soul."
PSALM 25, VERSE 2

"O Lord, open my lips, and my mouth shall show forth your praise."
PSALM 51, VERSE 15

"Make haste to help me, O Lord!"
PSALM 70, VERSE 1

NEW KING JAMES VERSION

O Prince of Peace, to all who receive
you, you bright light and peace.
Help me to live in daily contact with
you, listening to the words you have
spoken and obeying them.
O divine child, I place my hands
in yours; I shall follow you.
Oh, let your divine life flow into me.

SAINT TERESA BENEDICTA
OF THE CROSS

Three short graces to pray before eating

Lord Jesus, be our holy guest, our morning joy, our evening rest. While we enjoy our daily bread, impart your love and peace to every heart. Amen.

Blessed are you, O Lord. Fill our hearts with joy and gladness; that, always having enough, we may abound in every good work, in Christ Jesus our Lord, Amen.

For what we are about to receive, may the Lord make us truly grateful. Amen.

A short prayer to say in the evening by Saint Elizabeth of the Trinity

Dear Lord, give peace to my soul; make it your heaven, your cherished dwelling-place and the place of your repose. Amen.

The *Angele Dei* – a traditional Guardian Angel prayer

Angel of God,
my guardian dear,
to whom God's love
commits me here,
ever this day,
be at my side,
to light and guard,
rule and guide.

Amen.

A traditional prayer for night

Now I lay me down to sleep;
I pray the Lord my soul to keep.
Thy love guard me through the night,
And wake me with the morning light.

Father, we thank you for the night,
And for the pleasant morning light;
For rest and food and loving care,
And all that makes the day so fair.
Help us to do the things we should,
To be to others kind and good;
In all we do, in work or play,
To grow more loving every day.
Amen.

REBECCA WESTON

Celtic prayer of the night

I lie down this night with God,
And God will lie down with me;

I lie down this night with Christ,
And Christ will lie down with me;

I lie down this night with Spirit,
And the Spirit will lie down with me;

God and Christ and the Spirit
Be lying down with me.

Trust in the power of prayer

"Place your hope in the goodness of God, and look for his aid; knowing that if we truly and sincerely turn to him, he will say to us: 'Here I am.'"

SAINT BASIL THE GREAT

*"When you pray, I will answer you.
When you call to me, I will respond."*

ISAIAH, 58:9,
GOOD NEWS BIBLE

"You will call upon me and come and pray to me, and I will hear you. You will seek me and find me, when you seek me with all your heart. I will be found by you, declares the Lord."

JEREMIAH, 29:12–13,
ENGLISH STANDARD VERSION

We pray, not to persuade God of something in the way a small child attempts to persuade a parent to buy sweets. Instead, we pray to remind ourselves that we cannot achieve a perfect life alone. By praying, we recognize that we need God.

“We need to pray to God, not in order to make known to Him our needs or desires but that we ourselves may be reminded of the necessity of having recourse to God's help in these matters.”

SAINT THOMAS AQUINAS

"Place your mind before the mirror of eternity!

Place your soul in the brilliance of glory!

Place your heart in the figure of the divine substance!

And transform your whole self through contemplation into the image of the Godhead itself, so that you may also feel what Jesus's friends feel as they taste the hidden sweetness which God himself has reserved from the beginning for those who love him."

SAINT CLARE OF ASSISI

Brevity is no barrier to prayer. When words fail make these simple pleas

Lord, I am here.

Lord, thank you.

Lord, help me.

Lord, forgive me.

Lord, protect me.

Lord, be with me.

Prayer makes the darkened
cloud withdraw,

Prayer climbs the ladder Jacob saw,

Prayer gives exercise to faith and love,

Prayer brings every blessing
from above.

ADAPTED FROM WILLIAM COWPER

"Come close to God, and he will come close to you."

JAMES, 4:8,
INTERNATIONAL STANDARD VERSION

To make our weak heart strong
and brave:

Send the fire:

To live, a dying world to save:

Send the fire today!

O, see us on your altar lay,

We give our lives to you today,

So crown the offering now we pray:

Send the fire today!

Send the fire.

Send the fire.

Send the fire, today!

WILLIAM BOOTH
Send the Fire

Prayers for healing and troubled times

O Lord, my Lord, I pray to you
with tears.

O Lord, my Lord, my merciful saviour,
save me as I perish.

O Lord, my Lord, who came to save,
deliver me from this trial.

O Lord, my Lord, who accepts
our weaknesses and bears our pain,
send down your peace upon my
troubled soul.

O Lord, my Lord, my joy, grant that
I may rejoice in your mercy.

FROM ORTHODOX TRADITION

The Serenity Prayer

God, grant me the serenity
to accept the things I cannot change,
courage to change the things I can,
and wisdom to know the difference.

REINHOLD NIEBUHR

"There are times in our lives when, partly through trouble and partly through questioning, the very power to pray may seem to have deserted us. Yet the dumb and perhaps involuntary appeal for help – the mere daily and hourly uplifting of our troubles and anxieties into the Father's hands – may be met by such daily and hourly solutions and deliverances as to give us a completely fresh sense of the meaning and value of prayer."

CAROLINE STEPHEN

O God our Father, hear me. I am trembling in this darkness. Stretch out your hand to me. Hold your light before me. Recall me from my wanderings. Being my guide, may I be restored to myself and to you, through Jesus Christ. Amen.

SAINT AUGUSTINE

"O Lord, from the depths of despair I cry for your help: 'Hear me! Answer! Help me!'"

PSALM 130, VERSE 1,
LIVING BIBLE

Known as *De Profundis*, the cry from the depths, we are not alone in needing prayer in our hour of darkest need. The psalm promises that God will save his people; there is never any need to despair, no matter how dreadful the darkness.

May the Father,

who created all things in the beginning, bless you.

May the Son of God heal you.

May the Holy Spirit enlighten you,

guard your body, save your soul,

direct your thoughts,

and bring you safe to the heavenly country,

where he lives and reigns,

God, in a perfect Trinity,

forever and ever.

SARUM PRIMER

God to enfold me,
God to surround me,
God in my speaking,
God in my thinking.

God in my sleeping,
God in my waking,
God in my watching,
God in my hoping.

God in my life,
God in my lips,
God in my soul,
God in my heart.

God in my sufficing,
God in my slumber,
God in mine ever-living soul,
God in mine eternity.

CELTIC PRAYER

"Listen to me, Lord, and answer me,
for I am helpless and weak.
Save me from death, because I am loyal to you;
save me, for I am your servant and I trust in you."

PSALM 86, VERSES 1–2,
GOOD NEWS BIBLE

O Lord our heavenly Father who knows our weakness. You promised not to lay anything on us that is more than we can bear. Help us to bear our illness patiently. Carry us in your protective arms until we are well again in body, mind and spirit. Amen.

*“The Lord is near to the broken-
hearted
and saves the crushed in spirit.
Many are the afflictions of the
righteous,
but the Lord delivers him out
of them all.”*

PSALM 43, VERSES 18–19
ENGLISH STANDARD VERSION

O Mary, you shine continuously on our journey as a sign of salvation and hope. We entrust ourselves to you, health of the sick, who, at the foot of the cross, were united with Jesus' suffering, and persevered in your faith. 'Protectress of the Roman people', you know our needs, and we know that you will provide, so that, as at Cana in Galilee, joy and celebration may return after this time of trial. Help us, Mother of Divine Love, to conform ourselves to the will of the Father and to do what Jesus tells us... Amen.

POPE FRANCIS'S PRAYER FOR THE SICK
TO MARY, MOTHER OF GOD,

A powerful prayer for healing

Heavenly Father, I thank you for loving me. I thank you for sending your Son, Our Lord Jesus Christ, to the world to save and to set me free. I trust in your power and grace that sustain and restore me.

Loving Father, touch me now with your healing hands, for I believe that your will is for me to be well in mind, body, soul and spirit. Cover me with the most precious blood of your Son, our Lord, Jesus Christ from the top of my head to the soles of my feet.

Cast out anything that should not be in me. Root out any unhealthy and abnormal cells. Open any blocked arteries or veins and rebuild and replenish any damaged areas.

Amen.

PADRE PIO

"Simon Peter replied, 'You are the Christ, the Son of the living God.'"

MATTHEW, 16:16

"She [Martha] said to him, 'Yes, Lord; I believe that you are the Christ, the Son of God, who is coming into the world.'"

JOHN, 11:27

"But the tax collector, standing far off, would not even lift up his eyes to heaven, but beat his breast, saying, 'God, be merciful to me, a sinner!'"

LUKE, 18:13

ENGLISH STANDARD VERSION

Based on these Bible passages, The Jesus Prayer has been used for centuries to invoke the name of Jesus. It offers a powerful easy-to-remember prayer to use in daily life and in times of acute anguish.

Learn the Jesus Prayer off by heart and use it as a source of comfort, allowing you to concentrate your attention on the Lord

Lord, Jesus Christ, Son of God,
have mercy on me, a sinner.

Lord, Jesus Christ, Son of God,
have mercy on me, a sinner.

Lord, Jesus Christ, Son of God,
have mercy on me, a sinner.

Lord, Jesus Christ, Son of God,
have mercy on me, a sinner.

Lord, Jesus Christ, Son of God,
have mercy on me, a sinner.

Praise and thanksgiving

"Is anyone among you in trouble? Let them pray. Is anyone happy? Let them sing songs of praise."

JAMES, 5:13,
NEW INTERNATIONAL VERSION

We thank you, God of heaven,
For all the joys that greet us,
For all that you have given
To help us and delight us
In earth and sky and seas;
The sunlight on the meadows,
The rainbow's fleeting wonder,
The clouds with cooling shadows,
The stars that shine in splendour—
We thank You, God, for these.

JAN STRUTHER

"In you, Father all-mighty, we have our preservation and our bliss. In you, Christ, we have our restoring and our saving."

JULIAN OF NORWICH

"How wondrous are the marvels of your love, We are amazed, we stammer and grow dumb, for word and spirit fail us."

SAINT TERESA BENEDICTA
OF THE CROSS

Praying for others

Praying for others, even those who have hurt us, is one way of following Christ's command to love one another.

"To make intercessions [prayers] for men is the most powerful and practical way in which we can express our love for them."

JOHN CALVIN

All this day, O Lord,
let me touch as many lives
as possible for you;
and every life I touch,
let your spirit quicken within,
whether through the word I speak,
the prayer I breathe,
or the life I live.
Amen.

MARY SUMNER

Fountain of love, Lord, love our friends and teach them to love you with all their hearts, that they may think and speak and do only such things as are well-pleasing to you; through Jesus Christ our Lord. Amen.

SAINT ANSELM

"A friend loves at all times."

PROVERBS, 17:17,
ENGLISH STANDARD VERSION

Use this beautiful proverb as a foundation of prayer for friends and for friendship. When friends disappoint, frustrate or anger, remember that *a friend loves at all times.*

A prayer for family life

God of compassion,
whose Son Jesus Christ,
the child of Mary,
shared the life of a home in Nazareth,
and on the cross drew the whole
human family to himself:
strengthen us in our daily living
that in joy and in sorrow
we may know the power of your
presence
to bind together and to heal;
through Jesus Christ our Lord.
Amen.

A blessing for our family

May God bless us,
that in us may be found love
and humility,
obedience and thanksgiving,
discipline, gentleness and peace.

“Raise your tiny hand, Divine Child, and bless these young friends of yours, bless the children of all the earth.”

POPE JOHN PAUL II

Some find it uncomfortable praying for individuals, as if God could possibly have favourites. Take heart from the words of Saint Paul to apostle Timothy, who encourages us to pray for everyone:

"I urge, then, first of all, that petitions, prayers, intercession and thanksgiving be made for all people."

1 TIMOTHY, 1:1,
NEW INTERNATIONAL VERSION

Remember, O Lord, this city where we live and every other city and country, and all the faithful who live in them. Remember, O Lord, all who travel by land or water, all that labour under sickness or slavery; remember them. Amen.

SAINT JOHN CHRYSOSTOM

Prayers for understanding

Shine in our hearts, O master who loves mankind, the pure light of your divine knowledge, and open the eyes of our mind that we may comprehend the proclamations of your gospels.

FROM THE GREEK
ORTHODOX LITURGY

Prayer for illumination

Take time to appreciate the profound idea that prayer is able to open the eyes of our mind. Consider that we have other ways of seeing, that our mind can see into another dimension. Using this as an anchor, pray for illumination.

Open the eyes of our mind.

Open the eyes of our mind.

Open the eyes of our mind.

"I your handmaid am young in age, and inferior in understanding... Give me, I pray, a teachable heart, that I may know what is acceptable before you at all times... Send from heaven the spirit of your wisdom, that he may lead me in all my doings. Fill my heart with a sense of this; may your true wisdom give knowledge and counsel and understanding from your mouth."

QUEEN ELIZABETH I

Like Queen Elizabeth I, ought we to pray for a 'teachable heart?' What would having a teachable heart mean? Perhaps it is a heart that is open to guidance, receptive to explanations and willing to learn from misjudgements and mistakes.

Dear Lord, give me I pray
a teachable heart.

Grant me, I ask of you merciful God:

Carefully to study
Rightly to understand
Perfectly to fulfil that which
is pleasing to you,

To the praise and glory of your name.

SAINT THOMAS AQUINAS

Don't overthink things! The Apostle James wrote:

"If any of you lacks wisdom, let him ask God, who gives generously to all without reproach, and it will be given."

JAMES, 1:5
ENGLISH STANDARD VERSION

Remember these words when buried in brain-befuddling work or study. Wisdom is available to those who ask for God's support.

The Hail Mary

Explore the Catholic practice of praying to specific saints. The most well-known prayer is the Hail Mary, directed to Mary, mother of Jesus.

Hail, Mary, full of grace,
the Lord is with thee.
Blessed art thou amongst women
and blessed is the fruit of thy womb,
Jesus.
Holy Mary, Mother of God,
pray for us sinners,
now and at the hour of our death.
Amen.

Praying to saints is known as 'intercession'. When praying to the saints, we do not worship them, but rather humbly ask for help. Certain saints are traditionally approached for specific needs.

- Saint Joseph of Cupertino, patron saint of those sitting exams.
- Saint Christopher, patron saint of travellers.
- Saint Anthony, patron saint of lost items.
- Saint Anne, patron saint of mothers and women in labour.
- Saint Francis, patron saint of animals.

"Let Your divinity shine on my intellect by giving it divine knowledge, and on my will by imparting to it the divine love and on my memory with the divine possession of glory."

SAINT JOHN OF THE CROSS

A prayer for understanding

"Just tell me what to do and I will
do it, Lord.
As long as I live I'll wholeheartedly obey.
Make me walk along the right
paths, for I know how delightful
they really are.
Help me to prefer obedience to
making money!
Turn me away from wanting any
other plan than yours.
Revive my heart toward you.
Reassure me that your promises are
for me, for I trust and revere you."

PSALM 119, VERSES 33–38,
NEW LIVING TRANSLATION

"Prayer lies deeper than thought."

CAROLINE STEPHEN

Prayer for protection on journeys

O Glorious Saint Christopher
you have inherited a beautiful name,
Christ-bearer,
as a result of the wonderful legend
that while carrying people across
a raging stream you also carried the
Child Jesus.
Teach us to be true Christ-bearers
to those who do not know Him.
Protect all of us that travel
both near and far and petition Jesus
to be with us always.
Amen.

When feeling lost and adrift, seek solace in Psalm 107. This vivid hymn of thankfulness for deliverance is a reminder that we are not the first to wander alone.

"Some wandered in the trackless desert
and could not find their way to a city
to live in.
They were hungry and thirsty and had
given up all hope.
Then in their trouble they called
to the Lord, and he saved them from
their distress.
He led them by a straight road to a city
where they could live."

PSALM 107, VERSES 4–7,
GOOD NEWS BIBLE

"Proceed with much prayer, and your way will be made plain."

JOHN WESLEY

"Who can tell what a day may bring? Help us, therefore, gracious God, to live every day as if it were to be our last."

THOMAS À KEMPIS

Nature and creation

"I will meditate of the beauty of thy glorious majesty, and thy wonderful works."

PSALM 145, VERSE 5,
GENEVA BIBLE

"I see your heavens resplendent with stars. How glorious you are, radiant with light! Eternity watches me by the rays of the distant stars. I am small, insignificant, but the Lord is at my side. Your right arm guides me wherever I go."

PRINCE BORIS PETROVICH TURKESTANOV

We praise you, Lord, for all
your creatures,

especially for Brother Sun,

who is the day through whom
you give us light.

And he is beautiful and radiant
with great splendour,

of you Most High, he bears
your likeness.

We praise you, Lord, for Sister Moon
and the stars,

in the heavens you have made them
bright, precious and fair.

We praise you, Lord, for Brothers
Wind and Air,

fair and stormy, all weather's moods,

by which you cherish all that you
have made.

SAINT FRANCIS OF ASSISI
Extract from the Canticle
of Brother Sun and Sister Moon

An adventure takes a wrong turn, courage fails and all hope seems lost. Let Psalm 107 be your prayerful guide back to the loving arms of the Lord.

" Their ships were tossed to the heavens

and plunged again to the depths;

the sailors cringed in terror.

They reeled and staggered like drunkards

and were at their wits' end.

'Lord, help!' they cried in their trouble,

and he saved them from their distress.

He calmed the storm to a whisper

and stilled the waves.

What a blessing was that stillness

as he brought them safely into harbour!"

PSALM 107, VERSES 26–30,
NEW LIVING TRANSLATION

For the beauty of the earth,
for the glory of the skies,
for the love which from our birth
over and around us lies.
Christ, our Lord, to you we raise
this, our prayer of grateful praise.

FOLLIOTT S. PIERPOINT

Pray outdoors

Jesus and his disciples prayed in isolated places: at sea, on the shore, on mountainsides, in gardens. There is no need for prayer to be limited to indoor spaces. Use God's creations as a background to prayer. Seek out forests, watersides and floral landscapes, in praise and thanksgiving for the beauty of this Earth.

"Before daybreak the next morning, Jesus got up and went out to an isolated place to pray."

MARK, 1:35,
NEW LIVING TRANSLATION

Be inspired by the prayer habits of Jesus. Step outside the daily routine, wake earlier, find a private place apart from others and begin to pray.

Practice praying outside by remembering to stop, watch and cherish

When walking in beauty make a habit of:

- **Stopping:** stop the movements, still the body and mind.
- **Watching:** look about you. Observe the creatures, the plants, the sky, the ground.
- **Cherishing:** cherish the pleasure the place brings to your senses and soul.
- **Praising:** praise the Creator for the wondrous world.

"His prayers were a grand uplifting of heart and soul, as if he had found God on the mountaintop, met Him face to face, and was pleading before Him, realizing in his soul both the greatness and the goodness of the Almighty Father."

KRUPABAI SATTHIANADHAN
Describing her brother's prayers

Repentance and forgiveness

Lord God,
we have sinned against you;
we have done evil in your sight.
We are sorry and repent.
Have mercy on us according
to your love.
Wash away our wrongdoing
and cleanse us from our sin.
Renew a right spirit within us
and restore us to the joy of your
salvation,
through Jesus Christ our Lord.
Amen.

BASED ON PSALM 51,
THE BOOK OF COMMON PRAYER,

Dear God, as I draw nearer to you, cleanse my soul. Take from my soul, malice. Take from my heart, deceit. Take from my actions, hypocrisy. Take from my eyes, envy. Take from my mouth, slander. I crave instead, pure spiritual milk.

PRAYER ADAPTED FROM I PETER,
CHAPTER 2, VERSES 1–2

O Lord, who has mercy upon everyone, take away from me my sins, and mercifully kindle in me the fire of your Holy Spirit. Take away from me the heart of stone, and give me a heart of flesh, a heart to love and adore you, a heart to delight in you, to follow and to enjoy you, for Christ's sake. Amen.

SAINT AMBROSE

What blissful news by messengers from heaven,

How Jesus' blood for our redemption flows.

See him with hands out-stretched upon the cross;

Immense compassion in his bosom glows.

ADAPTED FROM A POEM
BY PHILLIS WHEATLEY

We are encouraged to cast all our cares onto God

Using these ancient Greek words, *Kyrie Eleison,* can help us begin this, sometimes difficult, process.

Kyrie eleison.
Christe eleison.
Kyrie eleison.

Lord, have mercy.
Christ, have mercy.
Lord, have mercy.

Transcendant glory

O Lord who is the everlasting essence of things beyond space and time and yet within them. You who transcends yet pervades all things, manifest yourself to us, feeling after you, seeking you in the shades of ignorance. Stretch out your hand to help us, who cannot without you come to you; and reveal yourself to us, who seek nothing beside you; through Jesus Christ our Lord.

JOHN SCOTUS ERIUGENA

Fill our hearts with joy and gladness, that we, always having all sufficiency in all things, may desire to every good work in Christ Jesus our Lord.

FROM THE CLEMENTINE LITURGY

Repeat these words until you find yourself smiling:

Fill our hearts with joy and gladness.

Fill our hearts with joy and gladness.

Fill our hearts with joy and gladness.

When praying an intense passage, it is spiritually nourishing to really take to heart just a few words. Let these words tumble around in your mind until they reveal their true meaning. Let these words then settle in your heart and speak to you every day.

Revive my heart toward you.

Revive my heart toward you.

Revive my heart toward you.

Grant me, even me, my dearest Lord, to know you. To love you. To rejoice in you. And, if I cannot do these perfectly in this life, let me at least advance to higher degrees every day, till I can come to do them in perfection. Let the knowledge of you increase in me here, that my heart may become full.

SAINT AUGUSTINE

The smallest word has meaning

When praying, imagine each word is written in gold. Even the smallest word delivered to God in heaven carries weight and meaning. No matter how tiny and whispered, each word is heard. Sometimes, repeating a simple prayer but placing careful emphasis on different words can unfurl a whole new understanding of what it is you are seeking or praising.

"Almighty God, we call you, the fountain of everlasting light. We ask you to send your truth into our hearts and to pour upon us the glory of your brightness."

SARUM BREVIARY

During and after prayer, visualize this idea of God's brightness being poured onto you. Is it possible to act afterwards in such a way that demonstrates this inner, glorious brightness?

Eternal God, primal light, maker of all created things, fountain of pity, sea of bounty, fathomless deep of loving-kindness: lift up the light of your countenance upon us! Lord, shine in our hearts, true sun of righteousness, and fill our souls with your beauty.

SAINT BASIL THE GREAT

Praying for virtues

Dear Lord, help me to clothe myself with compassion, kindness, humility, gentleness and patience. Help me to bear with my friends, family, colleagues and neighbours and forgive as I have been forgiven. Over everything, help me to put on love, which binds all together in perfect unity.

PRAYER BASED ON COLOSSIANS,
CHAPTER 3, VERSES 12–14,
NEW INTERNATIONAL VERSION

When Saint Paul wrote to a growing group of Christians in Colossae, he asked that they clothe *themselves* with a number of virtues. Be inspired by the idea and contemplate how these virtues will support your day-to-day spiritual and practical life.

Compassion
Kindness
Humility
Gentleness
Patience
Love

“ Make every effort to add to your faith goodness; and to goodness, knowledge; and to knowledge, self-control; and to self-control, perseverance; and to perseverance, godliness; and to godliness, mutual affection; and to mutual affection, love. For if you possess these qualities in increasing measure, they will keep you from being ineffective and unproductive in your knowledge of our Lord Jesus Christ.”

2 PETER, 1:5–9,
NEW INTERNATIONAL VERSION

The power of silent prayer

"True prayer is measured by weight, not by length. A single groan before God may have more fullness of prayer in it than a fine oration of great length."

CHARLES SPURGEON

What can I give him, poor as I am?

If I were a shepherd I would bring
a lamb;

If I were a wise man I would do
my part,

Yet what I can I give him
– give my heart.

CHRISTINA ROSSETTI
From 'In the Bleak Midwinter'

If words don't come easily when praying, Psalm 131 may resonate

"*My heart is not proud, Lord,*
my eyes are not haughty;
I do not concern myself with great matters
or things too wonderful for me.
But I have calmed and quieted myself, I am like a weaned child with its mother;
like a weaned child I am content."

PSALM 131, VERSE 1–2,
NEW INTERNATIONAL VERSION

"God speaks to me in the great silence of the heart."

SAINT AUGUSTINE

When resting in silent prayer, listen

Let us be attentive.

Let us be attentive.

Let us be attentive.

"When prayers don't spring to our lips, when our souls feel barren, when our hearts are forlorn and our mouths empty of praise, remember that God already knows our minds.

You have searched me, Lord,
and you know me.
You know when I sit and when I rise;
you perceive my thoughts from afar.
You discern my going out and my
lying down;
you are familiar with all my ways.
Before a word is on my tongue
you, Lord, know it completely."

PSALM 139, VERSES 1-4,
NEW INTERNATIONAL VERSION

"It matters little what form of prayer we adopt or how many words we use. What matters is the faith which lays hold on God, knowing that he knows our needs before we even ask him. That is what gives Christian prayer its boundless confidence and its joyous certainty."

DIETRICH BONHOEFFER

"I have wandered away like a lost sheep; come and find me."

PSALM 119, VERSE 176,
NEW LIVING BIBLE

"If you should beg God for a thing and he is slow to answer your prayer speedily, do not grieve, for you are not wiser than God."

SAINT ISAAC THE SYRIAN

“You may fear that the Lord has passed you by, but it is not so: he who counts the stars, and calls them by their names, is in no danger of forgetting his own children. He knows your case as thoroughly as if you were the only creature he ever made, or the only saint he ever loved. Approach him and be at peace.”

CHARLES SPURGEON

Seek peace in prayer

When trembling with fear, when defeated by sadness, when worried that hope is lost, give yourself permission to seek peace in prayer.

Approach God and be at peace.

Approach God and be at peace.

Approach God and be at peace.

The life everlasting

Facing our own mortality in prayer can be a frightening experience. But knowing that one day will be our last can help us treat every day as a precious gift. By looking at our end of days, we are better able to sanctify our present.

May he support us all the day long
till the shades lengthen
and the evening comes
and the busy world is hushed
and the fever of life is over
and our work is done.
Then in his mercy
may he give us a safe lodging
and a holy rest
and peace at the last.

JOHN HENRY NEWMAN

Take from our souls the strain
and stress
And let our ordered lives confess
The beauty of your peace.

JOHN GREENLEAF WHITTIER

As we lay us down to sleep,
We pray the Lord our souls to keep.
Watch and guard us through the night,
And wake us with the morning light.
Amen.

CHILDREN'S BEDTIME PRAYER

Watch, dear Lord, those who wake,
or watch, or weep to night,

Give your angels charge over those
who sleep.

Tend your sick ones, O Lord Christ.

Rest your weary ones.

Bless your dying ones.

Soothe your suffering ones.

Pity your afflicted ones.

Shield your joyous ones.

And all, for your love's sake. Amen.

SAINT AUGUSTINE

O Lord, the hard-won miles
Have worn my stumbling feet:
Oh, soothe me with your smiles,
And make my life complete.
The thorns were thick and keen
Wherever I trembling trod;
The way was long between
My wounded feet and God.
Where healing waters flow
To you my footsteps lead.
My heart is aching so;
Your gracious balm I need.

PAUL LAURENCE DUNBAR

O Jesus do not abandon me.
Into your hands, O Lord I commit
my spirit. O Blessed Mother Mary
help me.

SAINT DEVASAHAYAM PILLAI

May the Lord bless you
  and protect you.
May the Lord smile on you
  and be gracious to you.
May the Lord show you his favour
  and give you his peace.

AARON'S BLESSING,
CHAPTER 6, VERSES 24–26,
NEW LIVING TRANSLATION

It is in giving that we receive,

It is in pardoning that we are pardoned,

And it is in dying that we are born to eternal life.

SAINT FRANCIS OF ASSISI

PEOPLE QUOTED

Saint Ambrose, c. 339–397, Bishop of Milan

Saint Anselm, 1033/4–1109, Archbishop of Canterbury, theologian and philosopher

Saint Augustine, 354–430, Bishop of Hippo

Saint Basil the Great, c. 329–379, Bishop of Caesarea, theologian and Doctor of the Church

Saint Bede (the Venerable), 673–735, English monk and author

Prince Boris Petrovich Turkestanov, 1876–1934?, Orthodox bishop and confessor under Soviet persecution

Caroline Stephen, 1834–1909, Quaker writer and philanthropist

Saint Catherine of Siena, 1347–1380, Italian mystic

Charles Kingsley, 1819–1875, English clergyman, novelist and social reformer

Charles Spurgeon, 1834–1892, English Baptist preacher

Christina Rossetti, 1830–1894, English poet

Saint Clare of Assisi, 1194–1253, Italian founder of the Poor Clares

Saint Columba, 521–597, Irish missionary monk and founder of Iona

Saint Devasahayam Pillai, 1712–1752, Indian Catholic layman and martyr

Dietrich Bonhoeffer, 1906–1945, German Lutheran pastor, theologian and anti-Nazi dissident

Saint Dimitri of Rostov, 1651–1709, Russian bishop, hagiographer and preacher

Queen Elizabeth I, 1533–1603, English monarch

Saint Elizabeth of the Trinity, 1880–1906, French Carmelite nun and mystic

Emily Dickinson, 1830–1886, American poet

Folliott S. Pierpoint, 1835–1917, English writer and poet

Pope Francis (Jorge Mario Bergoglio), 1936–2025, Latin American pope

Francis de Sales, 1567–1622, Bishop of Geneva

Saint Francis of Assisi, 1181/2–1226, Italian founder of the Franciscans

Saint Ignatius of Loyola, 1491–1556, Spanish founder of the Jesuits

Saint Isaac the Syrian (Isaac of Nineveh), 7th century, Assyrian bishop and mystic

Jan Struther, 1901–1953, English writer and poet

Jarena Lee, 1783–1864, pioneering African American preacher and writer

Johann Sebastian Bach, 1685–1750, German composer

John Bunyan, 1628–1688, English Puritan preacher

John Calvin, 1509–1564, French theologian and reformer

Saint John Chrysostom, 347–407, Archbishop of Constantinople (Istanbul)

John Colet, 1467–1519, English priest and educational pioneer

John Donne, 1572–1631, English poet and cleric

John Greenleaf Whittier, 1807–1892, American Quaker, poet and abolitionist

John Henry Newman, 1801–1890, English theologian, cardinal and convert

Saint John of the Cross, 1542–1591, Spanish priest

John Scotus Eriugena, c. 815–877, Irish philosopher

John Wesley, 1703–1791, English founder of Methodism

Pope John Paul II (Karol Wojtyła), 1920–2005, Polish pope

Julian of Norwich, 1342/3–after 1416, English anchoress

Krupabai Satthianadhan, 1862–1894, Indian Christian convert and writer

Martin Luther, 1483–1546, German theologian and Protestant Reformer

Mary Sumner, 1828–1921, English founder of the Mothers' Union

Saint Meletius the Confessor, 4th century, Christian bishop

Narayan Vaman Tilak, 1861–1919, Marathi poet and Christian convert

Padre Pio, 1887–1968, Italian Capuchin friar and mystic

Paul Laurence Dunbar, 1872–1906, African American poet

Phillis Wheatley, 1753–1784, African American poet

Rebecca Weston, 19th century, American educationalist

Sadhu Sundar Singh, 1889–c. 1929, Indian Christian mystic

Saint Teresa Benedicta of the Cross (Edith Stein), 1891–1942, German-Jewish philosopher, Carmelite nun and martyr

Saint Teresa of Avila, 1515–1582, Spanish Carmelite nun, mystic and Doctor of the Church

Theodorus Studita (Theodore the Studite), 759–826, Byzantine monk and theologian

Saint Thérèse of Lisieux, 1873–1897, French Carmelite nun and Doctor of the Church

Thomas à Kempis, c. 1380–1471, German canon and author of *The Imitation of Christ*

Saint Thomas Aquinas, c. 1225–1274, Italian Dominican theologian and Doctor of the Church

William Booth, 1829–1912, English founder of the Salvation Army

William Cowper, 1731–1800, English poet and hymnwriter

BOOKS CONSULTED

The Bible, various translations

The Book of Common Prayer, Thomas Cranmer, 1549

Catherine Booth: A Sketch, Mildred Duff, 1914

The Christian Poet of Maharashtra, by J.C. Winslow, 1923

Collected Works of Charles Kingsley, 1890

Collected Works of John Wesley, 1826

Daily Devotions. Or the Christian's morning and evening sacrifice. Digested into prayers and meditations, for every day in the week, and other occasions, John Colet, 1684

The Dialogue of Saint Catherine of Siena, 14th century

Elizabeth I Collected Works, University of Chicago Press, 2000

Francis and Clare, the complete works, Paulist Press, 1982

Institutes of the Christian Religion, John Calvin, 1536

The Life and Religious Experience of Jarena Lee, Jarena Lee, 1836

Light Arising: thoughts on the central radiance, Caroline Emelia Stephen, 1908

Poems on Various Subjects, Religious and Moral, Phillis Wheatley, 1773

Prayers of the Early Church, edited by J. Manning Potts, The Upper Room, 1953

Prayers of the Middle Ages, edited by J. Manning Potts, The Upper Room, 1954

Prayers for the use of families, Albert Barnes, 1850

Saguna: A Story of Native Christian Life, Krupabai Satthianadhan, 1895

Service and Prayers for Church and Home, edited by Wilbur Patterson Thirkield, Methodist Book Concern, 1918

Summa Theologica, Thomas Aquinas, 13th century

Managing Director, Publishing Sarah Lavelle
Publisher Kate Pollard
Commissioning Editor Phoebe Bath
Assistant Editor Harriet Thornley
Words Joanna Gray
Series Designer Emily Lapworth
Head of Production Stephen Lang

Quadrille, Penguin Random House UK, One Embassy Gardens, 8 Viaduct Gardens, London SW11 7BW

Quadrille Publishing Limited is part of the Penguin Random House group of companies whose addresses can be found at global.penguinrandomhouse.com

Penguin Random House UK

Published by Quadrille in 2026

www.penguin.co.uk

A CIP catalogue record for this book is available from the British Library

ISBN 978-1-80712-114-3
10 9 8 7 6 5 4 3 2 1

Printed in China by RR Donnelley Asia Printing Solution Limited

The authorized representative in the EEA is Penguin Random House Ireland, Morrison Chambers, 32 Nassau Street, Dublin D02 YH68.